STANLEY BAXTER'S SUBURBAN SHOCKER

Featuring Rosemary Morningside and
the Garrulous Glaswegian Mr Ballhead

Stanley Baxter

with

Alex Mitchell

Illustrated by Weef

WATERFRONT

incorporating Paul Harris Publishing

First published 1985 by
Waterfront incorporating Paul Harris Publishing
Leith
Edinburgh

ISBN 0 86228 113 X

Printed in Scotland by John G Eccles Printers Ltd, Inverness

CONTENTS

Preface

Preface

That formidable suburban lady, Rosemary Morning-side, swept into my collection of characters a couple of decades ago. Since then she has made her presence felt in quite a few of my theatre, radio and television shows.

She speaks with the genteel accent that is carefully cultivated by many matrons dwelling in those suburbs of Edinburgh and Glasgow known as "exclusive". The vowels are flattened so that "My, you are flying high!" becomes "Mai, you are flaying hai!" and the saying "Is that a fact?" is rendered "Is thet a fect?" Occasionally she employs a Scotticism to add weight to her words.

Rosemary is not at all self-conscious and doesn't know the meaning of tact. Her airy, even genial, frank-ness is usually disconcerting to those with whom she comes in contact.

In complete contrast to Rosemary is Mr. John Ball-head, a self-educated and self-confident Glaswegian of the type sometimes encountered in our native hostel-ries. He is a Mr. Malaprop, holding forth with verbosity on all sorts of topics.

I present these two disparate Scottish characters in a series of situations, most of which are, to say the least, verging on the bizarre.

Stanley Baxter

1

Impatient Patient

As the result of a fall Ena lay in a hospital bed with a leg injury. The limb, heavily bandaged, was in traction.

She was in extremely low spirits and wailingly complained to a nurse.

ENA:

I seem to have been lying here for ages! Shall I EVER get out of this hospital.

NURSE:

Now, now, you must have patience. You received quite a shock when you fell. What you need now is complete rest and quiet.

ROSEMARY APPEARS.

ROSEMARY:

There you are, Ena! Ai knew you'd be needing some cheering up, so here Ai am! You'll be dying to know what's doing in the draive . . . Perhaps Ai shouldn't use the word "dying". You do look frightfully pale, dear . . . But let's forget about death. Ai've a wee bit of interesting news for you. It's about your friend, Clare Allbark.

ENA:

What is it?!

ROSEMARY:	Her husband's divorced her . . . for cruelty!
ENA:	I don't believe it!
ROSEMARY:	It's true, dear. Ai know you've always admired Mrs. Allbark, but Ai'm not naive. Ai knew she was rather mean. It transpired that she was always giving her husband that dog food to eat — Pal Meat. She made him Pal Meat stew, Pal Meat pie, quiche made from Pal Meat. She even gave him Pal Meat sandwiches to take to the office in his briefcase. In fact he ate so much Pal Meat that he couldn't pass a lamp post without lifting his leg.
ENA:	Rosemary, do you want to turn my stomach?
ROSEMARY:	No, dear. Better get the nurse to do that. Ai don't know how to work that contraption.
ENA:	(GROANS) Oh, never mind!
ROSEMARY:	Now Ena, you must stop feeling sorry for yourself. It's not as if there was anything organically wrong with you and you cope quite well with your migraine and your chilblains and those wee twinges of sciatica you have at times. You know, you're really very lucky being inside in weather like this. We've had a dreadful week of rain. The water was rushing down the draive in a torrent! . . . It's strange

	seeing your garden under three feet of water.
ENA:	WHAT?
ROSEMARY:	Och you don't need to worry. The water's seeping away. It's a good thing those big cracks appeared in your draiveway. Nature's drains! . . . Ena dear, would it not be better if you put some make-up on? (PEERS INTO ENA'S FACE) Oh you ARE wearing make-up . . . Ai must do up MAI face a little. Have you a mirror?
	ENA TAKES HAND-MIRROR FROM TOP OF THE BEDSIDE LOCKER. SHE IS ABOUT TO HAND IT TO ROSEMARY WHEN IT FALLS ON THE FLOOR AND SMASHES.
ENA:	Oh my GOD!
ROSEMARY:	Keep calm, dear. Seven years' bad luck shouldn't trouble you TOO much. You've always been an unlucky person.
ENA:	You can say that again.
ROSEMARY:	Uh huh . . . It's unfortunate that you won't be able to attend your niece Donna's wedding. Ai was at her show of presents last Tuesday. The wee carriage clock you sent her looked quite nice alongside the three bigger and more expensive carriage clocks she got. . . . Ai thought Donna looked quite well . . . But Ai think her daddy's

	a bit peeved that she's making him a grandfather next month . . . Oh, that reminds me — he's had a little spot of bother with the police.
ENA:	(SHOCKED) My brother Derek!? What kind of trouble?
ROSEMARY:	Och nothing much. He just forgot to get a licence for his shotgun.
ENA:	I see . . . Oh here's the doctor. ANCIENT DOCTOR SHUFFLES INTO THE WARD AND MAKES FOR ENA'S BEDSIDE.
ROSEMARY:	Good Lord, it's old Dr. McNutt! Ai thought he'd retired YEARS ago! He must be over ninety. (WITH SUDDEN CONCERN) Ena, do you think you're safe in his hands? You hear of doctors making mistakes sometimes, amputating perfectly sound limbs and . . . Good afternoon, doctor! Come to have a look at our patient?
DOCTOR:	She seems to be doing pretty well. (TAKES ENA'S PULSE)
ROSEMARY:	Poor Ena! She was having such fun at the party before the accident happened.
DOCTOR:	(GRIMLY) Was she?
ROSEMARY:	She certainly was! Ai'll never forget the way she danced the can-can with a bottle of gin in each hand. Then all of a sudden she slipped off the coffee-table. What a disaster! Two bottles of gin smashed to pieces!

6

DOCTOR:	(TO ENA) I'll lower the leg a little. HE ADJUSTS THE TRACTION SLIGHTLY.
ROSEMARY:	What happens if you pull this? SHE PULLS THE CORD AND ENA'S PLASTERED LEG RISES SUDDENLY TILL IT IS ALMOST VERTICAL. Oh, isn't that comical!
DOCTOR:	Stop that! Don't do that again!
ROSEMARY:	Come, come now, doctor! Where's your sense of humour? Don't be an old spoilsport!
DOCTOR:	Madam, I think you should leave this ward.
ROSEMARY:	(HUFFILY) Very well, if you insist that Ai should desert mai friend, Ai'll . . . Oh no, Ai can't leave yet! Ena. Ai came here specially to tell you something. Ai was so busy trying to cheer you up that it quite slipped mai mind!
ENA:	(WEARILY) What is it NOW?
ROSEMARY:	Ena, you may have been wondering whai your husband hasn't been to see you in the past four days.
ENA:	I haven't been wondering. He's had to attend a business conference in London.
ROSEMARY:	No, dear. He's on holiday at Peebles.
ENA:	On holiday? At Peebles? What on earth's he doing there?
ROSEMARY:	I don't know, dear. You'd have to ask that blonde au pair girl who's been staying next door to you.

7

Bizarre Bazaar

Ena was not too happy when she was put in charge of the clothing stall at the church bazaar. As she arranged the various garments donated by the members of the congregation she grumbled to her assistant, Maureen.

ENA: This is the third year I've been stuck at the clothing stall. It's such a bore. I'm fed up trying to sell this cast-off stuff. ROSEMARY OVERHEARS THIS AS SHE APPROACHES THE STALL.

ROSEMARY: Now, now, Ena, you mustn't complain. You know what happened that year when you were in charge of the bottle stall . . . Of course, you weren't to know that Mrs. Purdie used rum when she made her elderberry wine. You know, Maureen, we'd no aidea why that large bottle of elderberry wine on the stall was half empty, not until Ena spoke to the minister's wife . . . Ena dear, where did you learn that quaint expression "Go and get stuffed"?

ENA: Well actually I . . .

ROSEMARY:	Listen, we can't stand here chatting all day. There's work to be done. What have we got this year? (FINGERS CLOTHES ON STALL) Huh, "Nearly new" did they say? Nearly new ten years ago. Oh, here's Angela Cowley's red mini-dress, the one that made her look like a walking pillarbox.
MAUREEN:	It's a very short dress.
ROSEMARY:	It certainly is. Still, it gave us a good laugh when Angela wore it. D'you think all that horse-riding she does has made her legs look the way they do?
ENA:	She IS slightly bow-legged.
MAUREEN:	Do you think so?
ROSEMARY:	Don't let's bandy words about her legs. Let's get on with the work . . . Here, what's this tent doing on the clothing stall?
ENA:	It isn't a tent. It's Mrs. Longbottom's donation.
ROSEMARY:	Och Ai should have recognised it! Big Laura Longbottom's kimono! Her husband bought it for her on his business trip to Tokyo. He really has the strangest sense of humour.
MAUREEN:	You shouldn't have told her it made her look like Big Daddy, the wrestler.
ROSEMARY:	No, Ai should have told her she looked like a big haddie in it . . . What's that you've got, Ena? . . . No, don't tell me! It's Jennifer Danby's wedding dress!

ENA:	How do you know that?
ROSEMARY:	The wine stains down the front of it, dear. Then there was that chimney sweep they brought to the church porch to give the bride a good luck kiss. When he saw her he demanded a pint of champagne first. That sweep was a dreadfully awkward fellow. Look where he put his hand when he kissed her. (TURNS DRESS TO SHOW A LARGE BLACK HANDPRINT ON REAR).
MAUREEN:	Jennifer always wanted to be married in white.
ROSEMARY:	Yes. "White for purity," she said . . . There was hypocrisy for you! SHE BECOMES AWARE OF MRS. BRAITHWAIT EXAMINING GARMENTS ON THE STALL.
ENA:	Can I help you?
ROSEMARY:	Ai'll attend to this lady . . . Good afternoon, Mrs. Braithwait. Ai heard your central heating was on the blink again. Mai husband sent those cowboys packing when they offered to mend ours on the cheap . . . Anyway, Ai've got the very thing for you to wear in that big cold house of yours — bedsocks! Here they are. Ai think these belonged to old Mr. McDade. He used to say "Cold feet, warm heart". A lively old soul, wasn't he, Maureen? D'you

11

	remember how he waylaid you in the conservatory at the Benson's party? The old lecher would make a pass at ANY woman, no matter how plain she was . . . But back to the bedsocks, Mrs. Braithwait. They look like size nine. Ai'm sure they'd fit you. Nice and cosy. Keep your hydrophobia at bay!
ENA:	You mean "hypothermia", Rosemary!
ROSEMARY:	Ena, Ai wish you'd stop butting in when Ai'm trying to make a sale!
	AS ROSEMARY ROUNDS ON ENA MRS. BRAITHWAIT STALKS OFF IN HIGH DUDGEON.
	Now, Mrs. Braithwait . . . Good gracious, she's gone! Do you see what you've done, Ena Fotheringham? You've lost me a good customer. Old Mother Courage has pots of money.
MAUREEN:	She's not THAT old. Babs Braithwait and I were in the same class at school.
ROSEMARY:	WERE you, dear? You look years younger than her . . . Two years anyway . . . Good heavens!
ENA:	What is it?
ROSEMARY:	At the cake and candy stall! It's Hercules the Bear! . . . Oh no, it's Karen Maclaren in a fur coat! When did she get THAT?
ENA:	Last winter. Her boss is very good to her. He bought her the coat . . . to keep her warm.

ROSEMARY:	To keep her quiet you mean . . . Is that Mr. Biddleton? Yes it is. He's redder in the face than usual. He's had one of his business lunches . . . Hello there, Mr. Biddleton! You're looking quite sunburnt. Going to buy something? Ai've got the very thing for you . . . a lovely tie. (HOLDS UP FLAMING RED TIE) It'll match your eyes.
MR. BIDDLETON	No . . . er . . . no.
ROSEMARY:	Well is there something else you'd like to see? MR. BIDDLETON LEERS AT MAUREEN'S CLEAVAGE
MAUREEN:	Really, Mr. Biddleton!
ROSEMARY:	(ASIDE TO ENA) Is that not disgraceful? He wants a strip-tease at a church bazaar . . . MAUREEN TURNS AWAY AND MR. BIDDLETON GRUNTS AND STAGGERS OFF.
ENA:	I'm sure he's a little tipsy.
ROSEMARY:	He's as drunk as a fiddler's thingmy. Even his glass eye is bloodshot.
MAUREEN:	Which one is his glass eye?
ROSEMARY:	The one with the innocent expression . . . Karen's coming over . . . How ARE you, Karen? Oh mai! You look dreadfully warm. D'you not think it's a wee bit unwise to wear a . . .
KAREN:	Look, I can't stay long, Rosemary. I

13

	just wanted to know how you were getting on. I've got to meet someone . . . (COYLY) Actually I'm having a big affair!
ROSEMARY:	ARE you? Who's doing the catering?
KAREN:	Och you! (GOES OFF IN THE HUFF).
ROSEMARY:	What's wrong with HER? Ask her the simplest little question and she takes offence.
	THE MINISTER, THE REV. MR. SPINDRIFT, ARRIVES AT THE STALL.
MINISTER:	Good afternoon, ladies! How are we getting on here? Making lots of money for the Church Repair Fund?
ROSEMARY:	We're doing our best, Mr. Spindrift. We're all hoping to see the end of the dry rot in your pulpit.
MINISTER:	Eh? . . . Ah yes, indeed.
ROSEMARY:	(IDLY PICKING UP A GARMENT) Mai goodness, French knickers! It's ages since Ai saw a pair of these. Ai wonder who . . .
ENA:	I donated them. I don't wear them nowadays.
ROSEMARY:	Ena! Don't tell me you're going about without any . . . Oh, Mr. Spindrift, Ai thought you'd gone. . . . Do you see anything that takes your fancy?
MINISTER:	Let me see . . . I must say you have quite a varied array of articles on your stall.

14

ROSEMARY: Yes, lots of ladies have turned out their drawers for you.

MINISTER: Really! . . . I would like a word with you in the vestry later. (STAMPS OFF).

ROSEMARY: Would you craidit that! Ena, your French knickers have turned him on! . . . Well, he's not getting ME into that vestry of his!

Diet of Dismay

Maureen, a rather well-uphostered lady, had decided to lose weight and was on a strict diet. She looked exceedingly glum as she sat in the tea-room.

It was an old-fashioned establishment with, on the table, a four-tier cake stand bearing an assortment of cakes, tarts and doughnuts.

MAUREEN: (TO WAITRESS) I'd love one of those strawberry tarts . . . But I mustn't. Just bring me a pot of tea and a water biscuit.

THE WAITRESS NOTES DOWN THE ORDER AND GOES OFF. MAUREEN'S RESOLVE WEAKENS AND SHE IS ABOUT TO TAKE A STRAWBERRY TART WHEN SHE HEARS A DREADED VOICE.

ROSEMARY: Maureen McGravie! It's you! Ai haven't seen you since Elsie Benson's wedding reception! Did you get home all right? But of course you did. They were rather lavish with the champagne. And Ai saw you enjoyed the

	meal too . . . It's just a good thing that husband of yours is a strict teetotaller.
MAUREEN:	(DRILY) Yes, quite.
ROSEMARY:	Elistair and Ai are having his managing director for dinner tonight . . . Oh mai! That makes us sound like a couple of cannibals! . . . Ectually the man's a bit of a rough diamond so Ai'll not be doing any of mai cordon bleu cooking. Ai've bought a steak pie. Have you tried Rumshaw's steak pies? They're absolutely delicious . . .
MAUREEN:	I'm not very keen on steak pie . . . Not now anyway.
ROSEMARY:	Oh but you'd love this one! The pastry just melts in your mouth! (SHE TAKES STEAK PIE FROM SHOPPING BAG AND HOLDS IT UNDER MAUREEN'S NOSE). Smell that, Maureen! Doesn't that make your mouth water?
MAUREEN:	(FEEBLY) Yes . . . yes. WAITRESS ARRIVES AND PUTS POT OF TEA AND WATER BISCUIT IN FRONT OF MAUREEN.
ROSEMARY:	Maureen McGravie, what on earth is this you're having? A water biscuit! Are you not feeling well, dear? Ai THOUGHT your eyes looked even more sunken than usual.
MAUREEN:	I'm quite all right . . . As a matter of fact I'm on a diet.
ROSEMARY:	Oh is THET it? You're very wise . . .

18

and brave too to face up to the long struggle that lies ahead of you. Fanny Cartright was only half your weight and SHE went on a diet. It took her seven months to lose half-a-stone . . . Fanny was on a TAIRRIBLY strict diet — prune juice, a laxative and desiccated coconut. She said it kept her going . . . You can guess where it kept her going to.

(SHE EXAMINES BOTTOM TIER OF CAKESTAND) Oh, mai favourite wee doughnuts! (TAKES DOUGHNUT AND STARTS TO EAT IT) It's lovely! Home-made. Trai one, Maureen.

MAUREEN: No, no, I've made my stern resolve.

ROSEMARY: (MISHEARING) You've made your stern revolve!? D'you mean you're doing that wiggling business with your derriere . . . aerobatics, or whatever they call it?

MAUREEN: No, no, I meant I . . .

ROSEMARY: Ah, here's Minnie with mai favourite Vesuvius cake!

WAITRESS PUTS HUGE CONICAL CREAM CAKE IN FRONT OF ROSEMARY.

This is absolutely scrumptious! You'd love it, Maureen . . . Ai once saw Brenda Spendlove eat four Vesuvius cakes one after another. Then her skin erupted. Mind you, she was rather

19

inclined to overeat a little at times. Her doctor put her on to a soda water diet. Ai remember going to Brenda's place one night and we drank a whole soda siphon each . . . Then we sat about gassing.

MAUREEN: Brenda was rather plump at school. But she was very clever. Didn't she have the dux award?

ROSEMARY: No, the duck's disease. Her rear end was even bigger than yours. It really began to get her down. She went to a psychiatrist, thinking he might get to the bottom of her depression. He diagnosed that she was suffering from the BBC.

MAUREEN: Suffering from the BBC?

ROSEMARY: Yes, the Big Bahookie Complex.

MAUREEN: I see . . . I think there's somebody over there who knows you.

ROSEMARY: Where?

MAUREEN: At the table in the corner. She keeps looking over at you.

ROSEMARY: Oh it's Jennifer Smallweed! Hello, Jennifer! How ARE you? You're looking awfully well. See you later. (TO MAUREEN) Actually she looks ghastly. Ai'd rather be overweight like you than skinny like her.

MAUREEN: She seems to be enjoying her meal.

ROSEMARY: Oh, as the French say, tenez votre wheesht! She eats like a horse as well as having a face like one. Ai had her over for lunch one day. Polished off mai huge quiche in seconds. It was the first time Ai'd seen sparks flying off a knife and fork . . . Ai think Ai'll have an eclair. (TAKES ECLAIR FROM CAKESTAND) . . . Good grief!

MAUREEN: What is it?

ROSEMARY: That woman who's just come in! Ai never thought it possible. She makes YOU look slim! She's a mountain of fat! . . . You know, her face seems vaguely familiar. Now Ai wonder who she is?

MAUREEN: (COLDLY) She's my sister.

ROSEMARY: Well fency thet! Ai THOUGHT Ai saw a likeness . . . (LOOKS AT WRIST-WATCH). Oh here, Ai must be going. Ai'm due at a luncheon. It's a seven-course affair. The annual get-together of the Trencherwomen's Food Appre-ciation Society. (SHE FUMBLES IN HANDBAG AND CALLS TO WAI-TRESS) Mai bill, please, Minnie. (TAKES BILL FROM WAITRESS) What's that? £3.87? Oh dear, Ai've nothing less than a £20 note! (THRUSTS BILL AT MAUREEN). Will you pay it, Maureen? Ai'll get it next time . . . Bai-bai, dear!

WEEF.

The Pain in Spain

While their respective husbands were attending a business conference in London Rosemary decided that she and her friend Ena should have a "wee break in the sun" on the Costa del Sol.

Their second day on the beach didn't go quite as smoothly as they'd anticipated. It began with the two ladies looking at snaps that they'd just had developed.

ROSEMARY: Here's a very good snap of you, Ena. In fact it's the best photograph of you Ai've ever seen.

ENA: Let me see . . . Och, I've turned my face away from the camera!

ROSEMARY: I know, dear. It's an AWFULLY good picture . . . Oh there's that awful Spaniard! Did you hear what he shouted at us as we passed him?

ENA: No. What?
ROSEMARY WHISPERS INTO ENA'S EAR
No, no, Rosemary! It wasn't THAT!
SHE WHISPERS INTO ROSEMARY'S EAR

ROSEMARY:	Oh Ai see. It was "PARAsoles to you". (CALLS TO PARASOL-HIRER) We've got our own parasol, thanks. Ai'll put it up now. SHE STRUGGLES AND FAILS TO PUT UP THE PARASOL. Is this not absolutely dayabolical! Ai paid umpteen pesetas for this thing. (EXAMINES HANDLE OF PARASOL) No blooming wonder it's being awkward! . . . "Made in the USSR".
ENA:	Give it a thump on the ground. ROSEMARY DOES SO AND THE PARASOL TURNS INSIDE OUT.
ROSEMARY:	Is that not a spite? We'll just have to . . . Oh Ena your legs!
ENA:	What's wrong with my legs?
ROSEMARY:	Ai don't mean they're too short for your body. It's the way you're displaying them. There's a man over there with a telescope. Spying on us quite openly! These foreigners have got the cheek of the devil! (SHE PRODUCES HUGE PAIR OF BINOCULARS FROM BEACH BAG AND LOOKS ACROSS THE BEACH WITH THEM) . . . He's still looking at us. What a disgusting sight! Great big body and tiny swimming trunks.
ENA:	(TRYING TO SNATCH THE BINOCULARS) Let me see! Let me see!

ROSEMARY:	(SEVERELY) Ena dear, Ai know we're on the Continent, but you'll have to curb these wee impulses of yours. We've got to remember we're British, you know. We don't want these other people to think we're . . .
	A BOY APPROACHES THE TWO LADIES.
BOY:	Camas? Camas? You want camas?
ROSEMARY:	I want WHAT?
BOY:	You lie down. I give you camas.
ROSEMARY:	Would you craidit that? He wants me to lie down! Away you go, you wicked little pervert! Go away at once before Ai send for the gendarmes or whatever they call themselves.
	THE BOY, MYSTIFIED, BACKS AWAY.
ENA:	I think he was just trying to hire us airbeds.
ROSEMARY:	That'll be HIS story . . . Oh here, your back's tairribly red! Is it not painful?
ENA:	No it isn't.
ROSEMARY:	It soon will be. You'd really have to be very careful with your type of skin. D'you remember how that wine you liked so much at Palma made you all mottled? And the mosquitoes at Riccione brought your skin out in large lumps. Ai'll never forget your face on that holiday. It looked just like a picture of the moon's surface! Oh well it gave

	us all a good laugh.
ENA:	Look, I just want to lie here quietly and get tanned.
ROSEMARY:	Tanned? Please yourself, dear ... They say that oil and vinegar's good for awkward skins. Brenda Spendlove tried it at Viareggio last year. She was lying on the beach completely slabbered with oil and vinegar when suddenly she was surrounded by a coachload of people from Lancashire. They thought they had smelled a fish-and-chip shop ... Gosh, that sun's hot! Still, it's nice and quiet now. Of course, the Glasgow Fair holiday hasn't started yet ...
	A VENDOR WITH TRAY APPEARS.
VENDOR:	Helados! Helados chocolate!
ROSEMARY:	What's he got there: (SHE RISES AND PEERS INTO VENDOR'S TRAY) Och, it's just choc ices. (TO VENDOR) That's what we get at the Odeon. D'you understand? The Odeon ... the pictures.
VENDOR:	Ah, pickchiz! Ver' nice pickchiz!
ROSEMARY:	Oh here we go again. They're all sex mad.
VENDOR:	Ver' nice pickchiz.
ROSEMARY:	No thank you. We don't need any pictures. Go away ... Away and suck one of your choc ices. It might cool you down.

THE VENDOR RETIRES, SHAKING HIS HEAD.

It must be the sun that gets them. We never have this trouble with men at Dunbar or North Berwick. Still, Ai'm quite enjoying it here.

ENA: I'm not too keen on the food at the hotel.

ROSEMARY: Neither am Ai, dear. The other night when you were resting in your room Ai had a wee rubbery thing for dinner and Ai asked the waiter what it was. Well, he started waving his arms about like mad. Ai thought he was having a fit! Then it dawned. He was trying to tell me Ai was eating an octopus!

ENA: Ugh!

ROSEMARY: Fancy giving anyone an octopus to eat! Ai felt like bringing it up before the manager.

THE VENDOR REAPPEARS

Oh it's back again . . . Ai told you . . . we don't want any choc ices.

VENDOR: No, no, no choc ices. Uzzer bizniss. I buy and sell nice special pickchiz. Ladies an' gentlemens making beeg love.

ROSEMARY: Oh you buy them too? All right (REACHING INTO BEACH BAG AND PRODUCING A PACKAGE) How many do you want?

Blithe Spiritualist

For a brief period Rosemary was interested in psychic matters and was convinced that she possessed strong mediumistic powers.

She held several seances at her home and to one of these she invited her friend, Ena Fotheringham, and two neighbours, Mr. Biddleton and Miss Dryburgh, a faded spinster. By chance Rosemary's Uncle Dudley dropped in.

As soon as she had seated the company round a table in the lounge Rosemary excused herself and went off. The visitors waited, each looking distinctly apprehensive.

ENA:	Where's she gone? You know, Mr. Biddleton, I'm not really interested in this spiritualist business . . .
MR. BIDDLETON:	Well actually I've never been to a seance before. I don't think it's quite my cup of tea.
ENA:	I'm just wondering if Rosemary really IS a medium. It's a risky sort of thing when amateurs try to . . .
	ROSEMARY ENTERS. SHE IS

	WEARING A BANDEAU WITH A LONG FEATHER STICKING STRAIGHT UP FROM IT.
ROSEMARY:	Sorry to keep you waiting! Ai always like to sit and meditate for a little before Ai begin . . . I must get another washer for that tap in the bathroom . . . Well, are we all ready for a wee shufti beyond the veil?
ENA:	(DULLY) Er . . . I think we are.
ROSEMARY:	You'll have to stop talking, dear. The people on the other side of the veil are just a teeny bit wary of strangers, you know. (PUTS HER HAND UP TO THE FEATHER) This is what Ai receive my messages from beyond on. It's mai antenna.
UNCLE DUDLEY:	(WAKING SUDDENLY) Aunt Emma? Is your Aunt Emma there?
ROSEMARY:	No, Uncle Dudley, she's not there. Have you forgotten the last spirit message you got from her? (ASIDE TO THE OTHERS) Aunt Emma wants us to put him into a museum when he pops off. She's always telling him to go and get stuffed . . . Well, anyway, let's see what's happening beyond the blue horaizon. (SHE PUTS HAND TO FOREHEAD) It's rather quiet on the other side tonight . . . Oh, what's this? "Clicketty-click . . . sixty-six" . . . Would you craidit that? Psychic bingo!

ENA:	Rosemary, are you sure you can do this sort of thing? I know you're good with the tea-leaves, but . . .
ROSEMARY:	This is another thing altogether, Ena. It's a power that was gifted to me, dear. It came to me in the night, after Elistair and Ai had had oysters and champagne and brandy at Robin Spendlove's bankruptcy party. Ai began to see things and now Ai'm quite a dab hand at it. The Madam Arcati of Auld Reekie! . . . Now Ai must trai to contact Sitting Bull.
MR. BIDDLETON:	Who is he?
ROSEMARY:	Sitting Bull's mai spirit guide. Red Indian, you know. The spirit world's absolutely hoatching with Red Indians. I don't think Mr. Enoch Powell would like THAT. But they're all out to help us. . . . Ah here's Sitting Bull now. Good evening, Mr. Bull! How are you tonight? In good spirits, I hope! I've brought along a few friends to have a wee word with you. (TO THE COMPANY) He's bringing forward a lady to meet us. I'll close mai eyes and see better. Right away Ai see the name 'Samson'. Yes, the lady is Mrs. Samson. Oh, she's trying to get through to you, Miss Dryburgh! Oh dear! Mrs. Samson looks angry! Her husband's

with her and he looks terribly embarrassed . . . He's fading away now. But Mrs. Samson is still there. She's pointing straight at you and saying something, Miss Dryburgh. Your first name isn't 'Delilah' is it? Mrs. Samson seems to think so. Now she's talking about a baby. Oh goodness! She says Mr. Samson was the baby's father but she wasn't its mother. Oh she's flounced off in the huff . . . Oh Ai've just remembered something, Miss Dryburgh, were you not Mr. Samson's secretary at one time? . . . Och well, never mind. You'd only be a mere girl then . . .

ENA: Rosemary!

ROSEMARY: What is it, Ena?

ENA: Your uncle! He's dozed off and something's coming out of his mouth! It's that stuff they get at seances . . . ectoplasm!

ROSEMARY: What? . . . Ectoplasm mai foot! The old glutton's stolen the children's bubble-gum again. Ai'll ectoplasm him!

SHE TAKES A BROOCH FROM HER DRESS AND JABS THE BUBBLE-GUM WITH THE PIN. UNCLE DUDLEY STARTS UP IN ALARM.

UNCLE DUDLEY: What have you done?

ROSEMARY:	Do you know what YOU've done? You've broken mai contact with the other world! . . . He's always doing that. The other night I was just getting through to Queen Victoria when he made the most awful sound. I'd told him not to eat cucumber with his baked beans. Her Majesty was absolutely livid. She turned to the Prince Consort. "To hell with this for a caper, Albert!" she said, "They're nothing but a crowd of Radicals!"
UNCLE DUDLEY:	I was never a Radical!
ROSEMARY:	Oh we know that. Go back to sleep and let me concentrate . . . Ah, here's Sitting Bull again. . . . Beg pardon, Mr. Bull? Yes, yes, there's an Ena here with us. Have you a message for her? Oh, you want to give her a wee word of warning?
ENA:	A WARNING?
ROSEMARY:	Please stop chattering, Ena . . . Sitting Bull's making strange signs. It seems that a wicked unscrupulous man wants to do you some harm. Isn't that exciting, Ena?
ENA:	I don't know any man who'd want to . . .
ROSEMARY:	I don't doubt that for a second, dear . . . Ah, your spirit guide says the danger will come this week-end!

33

ENA:	What nonsense! As a matter of fact I'm spending this week-end with Mr. and Mrs. Biddleton at Dunbar. Mr. Biddleton invited me: didn't you, Mr. Biddleton?
MR. *BIDDLETON:*	Er . . . yes.
ROSEMARY:	Ena, are you sure you were invited to spend the week-end with Mr. and Mrs. Biddleton at Dunbar?
ENA:	Of course I'm sure! I've just told you that Mr. Biddleton invited me.
ROSEMARY:	That's funny . . . Ai met Mrs. Biddleton this morning and she told me she was going to spend this week-end with her sister in Aberdeen. . . . Any more spicy gossip for us, Sitting Bull?

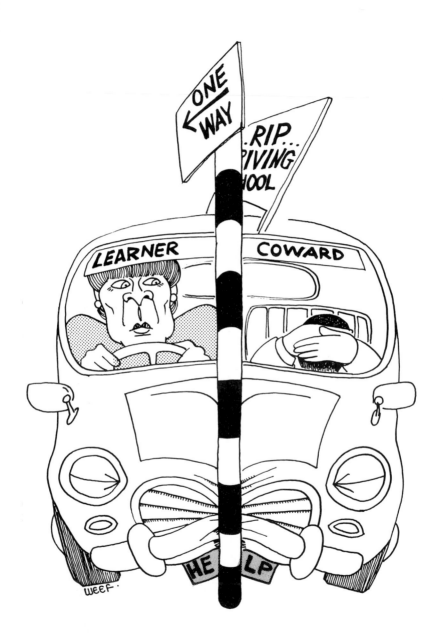

Driving Farce

Driving lessons were regarded by Rosemary as rather good fun. But for the various instructors who tried to teach her they meant utter frustration followed by sheer terror.

Embarking on her 13th lesson she was in her usual self-confident form. When she got into the car she found that the instructor was not the one she expected to see.

ROSEMARY: Well, all set for the Wall of Death? Just a little joke . . . Oh, you're the new man?

INSTRUCTOR: Yes, Mr. Pilchard was taken to a nursing home this morning.

ROSEMARY: Goodness me, not ANOTHER nervous breakdown! That's the fourth draiving instructor who's gone that way during mai twelve lessons. Mind you, Ai always thought Mr. Pilchard was a wee bit jumpy. Ai think the two tickets we got for reckless draiving preyed on his mind a little. And that wee crash with the Corporation bus didn't help . . . Och well, it's all in the day's work, isn't it?

INSTRUCTOR:	Er . . . quite. Right, starting drill.
ROSEMARY:	U-huh . . . On with the ignition!
INSTRUCTOR:	Engage the . . . clutch. CLUTCH!
ROSEMARY:	Clutch what?
INSTRUCTOR:	Into first gear.
ROSEMARY:	Ah yes . . . Awfully stiff, this handle. LOUD GRINDING SOUND.
INSTRUCTOR:	No, you shouldn't . . .
ROSEMARY:	It's all right. Safely away! CAR ROCKS VIOLENTLY That's the smoothest start Ai've made yet, Mr. . . . Here, you haven't told me your name.
INSTRUCTOR:	It's Coward . . . Reginald Coward.
ROSEMARY:	Golly! Not a very apt name for a draiving instructor.
INSTRUCTOR:	Look out! You're going to run into the back of that car in front!
ROSEMARY:	What car? D'you mean the one with the blue light on top? We'll soon pass it.
INSTRUCTOR:	No, no! . . . Oh, thank God! They've gone down the side street!
ROSEMARY:	That's a pity. Ai'd have enjoyed a race with them . . . Mai goodness, you're looking dreadfully pale! Tell you what . . . Ai'll draive you to a nice little bar Ai know and bai you a large whisky. After all, you're not draiving.
INSTRUCTOR:	No thanks. I think we should turn into Laburnam Drive. There's not much traffic there.

38

ROSEMARY:	Och not Laburnam Draive again! Ai hate the sight of those mangled railings.
INSTRUCTOR:	You've been there before? I suppose you were trying three-point turns.
ROSEMARY:	Three-point turns? Mr. Pilchard called them mai music hall turns.
INSTRUCTOR:	Did he happen to mention what side of the road you should drive on? At the moment we're on the right side, the WRONG side!
ROSEMARY:	How can it be the wrong side if it's the right side? Ai think you're trying to test mai reflexes, Mr. Fearty . . . er . . . Coward!
INSTRUCTOR:	To the LEFT!
ROSEMARY:	Okay. Keep your hair on. Oh Ai beg your pardon! Ai didn't mean to be personal. Anyway, Ai think bald men can look quite distinguished. Between you and Ai, Ai had quite a wee notion of Telly Sav . . .
INSTRUCTOR:	Please, to the LEFT!
ROSEMARY:	All right. Over we go.
	CAR SWERVES VIOLENTLY.
	Happy now, Mr. Coward? Did Ai draive over a traffic island just now?
INSTRUCTOR:	You're driving along the PAVEMENT!
ROSEMARY:	Am Ai? Ai wondered why that man jumped over a hedge into a garden. Don't worry. Ai'll get back on the road again.

INSTRUCTOR:	DO concentrate! Please!
ROSEMARY:	Ai AM concentrating. But this is becoming a wee bit boring. Let's have a bash at the motorway — the M1 or the M6 or whatever they call it.
INSTRUCTOR:	Never! Slow down for a left-hand turn two streets ahead.
ROSEMARY:	Here, are you in the huff?
INSTRUCTOR:	No I'm NOT in the huff.
ROSEMARY:	Thank goodness. Ai thought Ai'd done something to annoy you . . . Now then, we turn right.
INSTRUCTOR:	No, no! We shouldn't be in this street!
ROSEMARY:	Ai can see why. It's full of reckless draivers! Half those cars are on the wrong side of the road!
INSTRUCTOR:	It's a one-way street!
ROSEMARY:	Well Ai'm only going one way.
INSTRUCTOR:	Quick! Turn right before that policeman sees us. No, no, not up here!
ROSEMARY:	Whai not? It's rather a nice wee road. Look at the lawns on either side and those lovely flower beds.
INSTRUCTOR:	This is a private driveway! We're in somebody's garden!
ROSEMARY:	ARE we? Och well, maybe if we drop in on them they'll give us a cup of tea. CRASH OF BREAKING GLASS AS THE CAR SHOOTS INTO A CONSERVATORY. How's that for an emergency stop?

INSTRUCTOR: Oh my God! (HE LIES BACK IN A FAINT).

ROSEMARY: (PUTTING HER HAND OUT OF CAR WINDOW AND PICKING A FLOWER) Look at this gorgeous green orchid! . . . Oh, it just matches your face!

(SHE PUTS ORCHID ON INSTRUCTOR'S CHEST)

Trouble in Store

Ena, not the most cheerful person at the best of times, was trying on hats in one of the bigger stores. None of the creations met with her approval and she was most dispirited.

Great was her dismay when Rosemary put in an unexpected appearance.

ROSEMARY: Ena Fotheringham, it's YOU! Ai haven't seen you since the Licensed Traders' ball. Have you quite recovered?

ENA: Recovered? What do you mean?

ROSEMARY: Never mind. We'll draw a wee veil over that evening ... Is this you buying another hat?

ENA: I always buy a hat when I'm down in the dumps.

ROSEMARY: Oh is THAT where you usually get them? Well let's try the impossible and see if we can find something that suits you.

ENA: (PUTTING ON A PILLBOX-TYPE HAT) What about this?

ROSEMARY: Oh no, dear! That's just not you . . . It's funny how that wee hat makes your face look even bigger . . . Och let me have a shot at these hats. (SHE PUTS ON A FLAT WIDE-BRIMMED HAT) Oh, Joan Collins! Ai wore a hat like this, a brown one, when Ai was down at our country cottage. One day it blew off into a field where there'd been a cattle show. Ai had to try on seven before Ai found the right one . . . What on earth's this? (SHE PICKS UP AND PUTS ON A KNITTED CAP WITH FLOWERS ON IT).

ENA: It looks like a nightcap with dandelions on it.

ROSEMARY: Yes, it does. You wouldn't get ME to wear that in bed . . . Good grief, would you look at this monstrosity! (PICKS UP BUSBY-TYPE HAT). Only a loonie would go out with this thing on their head!

ENA: That's MY hat.

ROSEMARY: Whaaat? D'you mean this is what you were wearing when you came in here?

ENA: Yes . . . I bought it in London.

ROSEMARY: Ena dear, far be it from me to question your taste, but were you not just a wee bittie sloshed when you let them palm that hat off on you?

ENA: No, I certainly was not!

ROSEMARY: Oh well, it's a good thing you're below

average height ... Otherwise you might have been mistaken for a guardsman.

THE SHOP MANAGER APPROACHES THE PAIR.

MANAGER: Good afternoon, ladies. The assistant tells me you haven't found a hat to suit you yet.

ROSEMARY: And we're not likely to. Where on earth did you get this collection of horrible hats?

MANAGER: (NETTLED) I have no idea, madam. If you like I'll take you to the buyer.

ROSEMARY: To the BYRE? What do you think Ai am ... a COO? (TO ENA) Let's go over to that counter and have a look at the ski wear.

MANAGER: Ah, we can dress you from head to toe for the slopes.

ROSEMARY: No thanks. I can dress myself. Just let's see the ski gear.

MANAGER: Yes, madam. (TO GIRL ASSISTANT) Miss Henderson, get down your pants.

GIRL ASSISTANT GAWPS

ROSEMARY: (ASIDE TO ENA) There's definitely something kinky about him.

MANAGER: (IMPATIENTLY) Miss Henderson, bring the ski pants.

GIRL ASSISTANT BRINGS SKI PANTS ON HANGERS

ROSEMARY: These look quite naice.

MANAGER: Yes, they are made for allure!

45

ROSEMARY: For a WHAT? . . . Oh Ai see. Ai'd like to trai on a pair.

MANAGER: I'm afraid we don't have a fitting-room here.

ROSEMARY: Och don't worry about that. Ai'll just take off mai shoes and pull the pants up over mai dress.

MANAGER: Really, madam! I don't think you should try to put on the . . .

ROSEMARY: Whai not? Go away if you're afraid of being embarrassed. Anyway, you won't see anything you shouldn't. (SHE TUCKS FOOT OF DRESS INTO SKI PANTS) There we are! D'you not think they look very smart, Ena?

ENA: (WEARILY) Oh VERY.

ROSEMARY: (TO MANAGER) Now Ai'd like to see a pair of skis. Do you have them in stock?

MANAGER: Yes, we have. (TO GIRL ASSISTANT) Miss Henderson, skis, please.

ROSEMARY: Ai've always fencied ski-ing.

MANAGER: You'll require boots too, of course.

ROSEMARY: Well, naturally! You don't think Ai'd go scooshing about the Alps in mai stocking soles, do you? GIRL ASSISTANT APPEARS WITH PAIR OF SKIS. Just let me put mai feet in the straps . . . That's it . . . Oh Ai'm afraid Ai can't walk in them.

GIRL ASSISTANT HANDS HER A PAIR OF SKI STICKS.

Oh that's a good aidea!

MANAGER: I take it you're satisfied with the articles . . . Have you an account with us or do you wish to pay cash?

ROSEMARY: Oh Ai'm not buying these things!

MANAGER: You're not buying them! Then what are you doing here, wasting our time?

ROSEMARY: Can you not guess? Look outside!

MANAGER: Look outside?

ROSEMARY: Yes, you'll see whai Ai'm sheltering here . . . It's raining like hell!

Horror Film

Rosemary and her husband Alistair returned from Marbella with a lengthy film record of their holiday. They had taken turns at operating the film camera. Their friends, Tom and Ena Fotheringham, were invited to attend the premiere of the amateur epic.

ROSEMARY: Into the lounge, Ena dear. We've just got the films back from the developers and Elistair and Ai haven't seen them yet. Ai thought you'd like to share our wee picture show with us. . . . Elistair, have you not got your thing going yet? (TO ENA) He's always having trouble with his projector. (BRIGHT LIGHT SHINES SUDDENLY ON SCREEN).

ALISTAIR: There we are!

ROSEMARY: Thank goodness. Well, off we go! Memories of Marbella! You're going to enjoy this, you two . . . especially as you didn't get away yourselves this year. Ai was sorry to hear the appeal against your rates assessment failed. You know that lawyer you hired to

	handle it? We saw him and his family at Marbella . . . enjoying themselves on your money! . . . Now what have we here? Oh Ai took this film myself. It's just Elistair getting off the 'plane when we arraived. He's an awful fearty when it comes to flying. (TO ALISTAIR) You really shouldn't have started on that second bottle of brandy on the 'plane.
ENA:	Good heavens, he's fallen!
ROSEMARY:	It's all right. He managed to get up off the tarmac. In fact he was ready for another refreshment when we got to the hotel. The wine waiter gave him a cocktail called "Card Table".
TOM:	Why on earth do they call it "Card Table"?
ROSEMARY:	If you drink a couple your legs fold up . . . Oh here's Elistair's mother in front of the hotel. You remember, she flew over unexpectedly for the first week of our holiday.
ENA:	(POINTING AT SCREEN) Is that her over there?
ROSEMARY:	No, no . . . that's a heap of rubble. Mother-in-law is on the right, next to the bulldozer. The bulldozer's the one that's not moving . . . There goes mama up the steps towards the bar.
ENA:	Did the hot sun not disagree with your mother-in-law?

ROSEMARY: It wouldn't dare! . . . There she's trying to get into the taxi to go back to the airport. That's me helping her into it — with my foot . . . Now, who's this? Oh it's that little stout man from Surrey, Mr. Shortbottom. You know, Tom, he was your double! The same build and the shortness of breath. And HE was fond of his food too . . . Just look at him capering about with that funny hat on! He was in great fettle that day, the life and soul of the party. Next morning — dead. Went like that (SNAPS FINGERS).

ENA: Good gracious! What did he die of?

ROSEMARY: We weren't sure at first. Then Ai looked at Elistair and Elistair looked at me. "Salmonella" was written across our faces . . . Still, Mr. Shortbottom enjoyed his holiday. He was as brown as a berry when they crated him and sent him home . . . Huh, look at this!

ENA: Oh, twin mosques. I love those onion-shaped towers!

ROSEMARY: Those onion-shaped towers are attached to the body of Topless Teenie.

TOM: Who was she?

ROSEMARY: Just a blonde girl from the hotel. She always happened to be lying about the beach when Elistair was filming. Every time he took out his Rollieflex she dropped her bra. Oh here Ai am in mai bikini!

ENA: Hmmm . . . I'm afraid I wouldn't be brave enough to wear a bikini.

ROSEMARY: Ai can understand that, dear. But you're too sensitive about your legs. Those hollows you have in your thighs are quite normal at your age . . . Ah, there's Enrico. That's the Italian man who was staying at the hotel. He had a cine-camera too and he was always filming me! Elistair, have you got that film Enrico gave you?

ALISTAIR: (IMPATIENTLY) Yes, yes, I have it here.

ROSEMARY: Let's see it then . . . It seems Enrico was in the film business. He told me Ai was quite photogenic!

ALISTAIR: (SULLENLY) Here's the film.

ROSEMARY: Good! . . . Oh, it's much clearer than yours, Elistair! There Ai am in mai bikini again. That was the afternoon you went for a wee lie-down in the room and Ai went off to sun-bathe on mai own.

ENA: It's a VERY clear picture. Who's that in the background?

ROSEMARY: Who's WHO in the background? (PEERING INTENTLY AT THE SCREEN) Ai didn't know there was anyone in the background . . . Oh yes, Ai see someone now.

TOM:	It looks like that blonde from your hotel.
ROSEMARY:	Mai God, so it is! Lying there topless and shameless as usual.
TOM:	There's a chap lying beside her. He's leaning over her. Now he's looking up . . . Good heavens, it's . . .
ROSEMARY:	(ROUNDING ON ALISTAIR) It's YOU, you wicked thing! Ai thought you were back at the hotel having a wee lie-down. And there you were on the beach having a wee lie-down with that dreadful blonde! . . . Oh, I could kick maiself!
ENA:	Why, Rosemary?
ROSEMARY:	Because that afternoon Ai turned down Enrico's invitation to have champagne in his room!

Plane Talk

A 'bargain holiday' in Paris offered by Gorbals Airways appealed to Rosemary. She bullied her friend Ena into accompanying her on the trip.

Ena, terrified of flying, was highly nervous as they took their seats in the 'plane. Rosemary, as usual, was full of joie de vivre.

ROSEMARY: Here we are! Paris, here we come! . . .
              Are you comfy, Ena?

ENA: (DRILY) Oh, VERY . . . You know,
              Rosemary, I'd be much happier if we
              were going surface.

ROSEMARY: Going surface? That makes us sound
              like a couple of wee beetles. Now
              cheer up, dear. We'll be in Paris in just
              two HOURS! . . . barring accidents, of
              course. But it doesn't do to look on the
              black side. Trai to forget that you're
              accident-prone.

ENA: I'm trying to forget that.

ROSEMARY: That's the spirit! Think of all the naice
              places we'll visit when we get to Paris.

ENA: Uh huh . . . I must go the Louvre.

ROSEMARY:	(MISHEARING) Oh you can't go until the plane's in motion. Just be patient. (SHE TURNS AND ADDRESSES A STOLID SOBER-SUITED MAN SITTING ACROSS THE PASSAGEWAY FROM HER) Is this you taking a wee jaunt on your own?
MAN:	(SEVERELY) I'm going to Paris on business.
ROSEMARY:	Oh, we've heard THAT story before! Still, you're quite right to have a wee fling before you get any older.
MAN:	I assure you I'm going on business. Actually I'm an exporter.
ROSEMARY:	An ex-porter? Oh Ai see, you've retaired from British Rail. Do you hear that, Ena? This gentleman's a retired railway porter. (TURNING TO MAN) You can give us a hand with our luggage when we get to Paris . . . (SUDDEN BURST FROM PLANE'S ENGINES) Oh we're away! Up we go! (LOOKING OUT OF WINDOW) Look at those people down there. They're just like ants.
ENA:	They ARE ants. We haven't moved yet.
ROSEMARY:	Have we not? We were due to flai off ten minutes ago. Ai'll ask the stewardess. Ring the bell, Ena.
	ENA PRESSES BUTTON AND BELL RINGS LOUDLY. A TATTY-

LOOKING STEWARDESS SHAM-
BLES INTO VIEW.

STEWARDESS
(WEARILY):
Welcome aboard. Was you ringing?

ROSEMARY:
Would you listen to that! "Was you ringing"! (TO STEWARDESS) Ai want to know what's holding this plane up.

STEWARDESS: I've often wondered that maself.

ENA:
Just tell us . . . When do we take off?

STEWARDESS: Any minute now . . . Here's the pilot now.

VERY YOUNG PILOT WITH PEBBLE GLASSES STAGGERS ALONG THE PASSAGEWAY, YAWNING AS HE PASSES BY.

ROSEMARY:
Good heavens, he's only a boy! I wonder if he's got his O-levels . . . Maybe he should stay at ground level.

PLANE'S TWIN ENGINES ROAR INTO LIFE.

ENA:
We're moving! Oh Rosemary, I'm scared!

ROSEMARY:
You won't be scared for long, dear. They say that the take-off is the most dangerous part of the flight. We'll soon know . . . one way or the other. (LOOKS OUT OF WINDOW) Och, he's not such a bad pilot after all. He's managed to miss those multi-storey flats by inches. Now sit back and relax, Ena. Would you like a wee read? Here's an awfully interesting book

	(HOLDS OUT BOOK) 'The High and the Mighty'. It's all about a planeload of people who . . .
ENA:	No thanks!
ROSEMARY:	(PRODUCING CIGARETTE-CASE AND LIGHTER FROM HER HAND-BAG) We'll have a wee puff to settle your nerves.
STEWARDESS:	No, no. No smoking.
ROSEMARY:	What do you mean 'No smoking'? I MUST have a ciggie. Anything to get that smell of petrol out of mai nose.
STEWARDESS:	It's not MY fault the petrol tank's leaking.
ENA:	Rosemary, put away that lighter! Do you want to set the 'plane on fire?
ROSEMARY:	Of course not! Ai've no intention of setting the 'plane on fire. Really, Ena, you have the strangest ideas at times. (TO STEWARDESS) If we can't smoke can we have a wee bite to eat? Ai'd like a little scampi followed by crème caramel, then coffee and cream and some . . . Ena, what are you doing with that paper bag over your face? Just shut your eyes if you're afraid to look out of the window.
STEWARDESS:	(TO ROSEMARY) We don't serve meals. But I can give you sandwiches.
ROSEMARY:	Oh that'll have to do. Ai'm so hungry Ai could eat a horse!
STEWARDESS:	Eat a horse? In that case you'll enjoy our sandwiches.

MAN:	(TO STEWARDESS) I say, when exactly do we touch down at Paris?
STEWARDESS:	Two o'clock dead.
ENA:	Oh I wish people would stop talking about death!
ROSEMARY:	Keep calm, dear. (TO MAN) Is this not rather a slow flight?
MAN:	It certainly is! When I flew to Italy I left Glasgow at 8 pm and I touched Florence at midnight.
ROSEMARY:	I see. You've an Italian girl friend too. Ai think you're one of those international playboys!
CAPTAIN:	(ON INTERCOM) Ladies and gentlemen, owing to a slight technical fault we are having to divert the flight to . . . er . . . I'm not quite sure. Let me have another look at the map . . .
ROSEMARY:	A slight technical fault? What does that mean?
STEWARDESS:	(GROANS) Oh don't tell me the wheels have fallen off again!
MAN:	Heavens, we'll touch down with a tremendous thump if we make a belly landing!
ROSEMARY:	(ASIDE TO ENA) His belly landing would make a tremendous thump . . . Where are we now?
CAPTAIN:	(RADIO MESSAGE OVER INTERCOM) Ladies and gentlemen, you are now over the North Sea. If you look out of the windows on the left hand side

	you will see a little yellow dot on the surface of the sea.
ROSEMARY:	(LOOKING DOWN FROM WINDOW) Where is it? . . . Oh I can see it now! D'you see it Ena? What is it? A landmark?
CAPTAIN:	The little yellow dot is the rubber dinghy from which I am speaking to you.
ENA:	Oh my God! The pilot has baled out! We're going to crash!
ROSEMARY:	Not at all, dear! Every 'plane is fitted with an automatic pilot. It'll soon get us to Gay Paree! . . . What a good view we're getting of the sea now. You can see every ripple on the water.

WEEF.

Last Resort

Maureen is the owner/manageress of a small upmarket travel agency. When she had to go to a niece's wedding she intended to close the agency's office for the day.

Rosemary wouldn't hear of this and declared that she would deputise for her. Against her better judgement Maureen agreed. The first potential clients her deputy dealt with were a young couple, Jennifer and her fiancé Ian.

The office appeared to be deserted when they entered.

JENNIFER: We don't want to go to a terribly expensive place.

IAN: Oh hang the expense! I'm not going to skimp on our honeymoon . . . There's nobody about. (CALLS) Hello! Anybody here?

ROSEMARY, HOLDING CUP AND SAUCER, EMERGES FROM BEHIND A POSTER OF A MEDITERRANEAN SEASCAPE.

ROSEMARY: Oh hello! Ai was just having a wee flai cup in the middle of the Med! (PUTS

	DOWN CUP AND SAUCER ON COUNTER) Now then, what can Ai do for you? Were you thinking of having a wee holiday? (LEANS FORWARD AND PEERS INTO THEIR FACES) If you don't maind mai saying so, you could both do with one. You're both looking just a wee bit peelly-wally.
JENNIFER:	Actually we're getting married and we've been very busy in our flat.
IAN:	Yes, we've been hard at it.
ROSEMARY:	Have you? . . . Och Ai know what it is. When Ai became engaged mai fiancé and Ai spent HOURS in our flat. . . . We did some painting and papering too.
JENNIFER:	(COLDLY) We want to arrange our honeymoon. My fiancé was thinking of Interlaken.
ROSEMARY:	Mine could think of nothing else! (TO IAN) But where do you fency going on honeymoon?
IAN:	Well, my first choice would be . . .
ROSEMARY:	What about the Italian Riviera: Last year Ai was there with Elistair. That's mai husband. Ai rather liked it, but Elistair wasn't so keen. He wanted to lie on his tummy in the sun. Then he found that nothing would lie on his tummy. We got an awful lot of ravioli in that hotel. Elistair brought it up before the manager

JENNIFER:	I see . . . Have you any cruises?
ROSEMARY:	Ai think so . . . but. Well personally Ai wouldn't advise a cruise. WE went on a cruise for our honeymoon. D'you know what Ai'm going to tell you? For a whole week that husband of mine was hanging on to the rail of that ship with his stomach. Ai thought he was going to throw up the sponge.
IAN:	(LOOKING AT POSTER) I think Le Touquet might suit me.
ROSEMARY:	A toupee? Ai'm afraid we don't have such a thing here. But d'you really think you should bother with one? I always think that bald heads tan rather nicely.
IAN:	I was talking about Le TOUQUET.
ROSEMARY:	Oh it's quite jolly there. Full of French-men. But don't let that worry you. You can have a pleasant week-end there for £600 each.
JENNIFER:	It might be better if we went to Spain?
ROSEMARY:	Ah, sunny Spain! Your holiday should go with a bang there. Mind you . . . (LOOKS AT IAN'S RECEDING HAIR-LINE) . . . if you're partial to sunstroke it can be absolutely fatal. But we've a nice hotel on the Costa del Thingmy.
IAN:	It's a good hotel, is it?
ROSEMARY:	Yes, tairribly picturesque. Mai husand and Ai were there and it was amazing how quickly we became used to the lizards.

JENNIFER:	LIZARDS?!
ROSEMARY:	Uh huh, they're everywhere in that hotel. And the cockroaches were no great problem. They were always dead when you found them in your coffee. Anyway, we didn't have coffee very often. It was quite undrinkable.
JENNIFER	(SULLENLY) We'll have a look at some of the booklets.
	JENNIFER AND IAN STUDY BOOK-LETS
	ENTER TOM AND ENA, FRIENDS OF ROSEMARY.
ROSEMARY:	Mai goodness! Tom and Ena! What are you two doing here?
TOM:	What are YOU doing here, Rosemary?
ROSEMARY:	Advaising people where to go on holiday. It's great fun. Actually Ai'm helping Maureen. She's gone off to her niece's wedding. You know her niece Deirdre, the girl with the lovely face . . . Pity about her legs.
ENA:	Well WE'RE here for some holiday advice.
TOM:	Yes, we've a notion of going to Cannes.
ROSEMARY:	(SHOCKED) Cannes! Oh, it wouldn't suit you two!
ENA:	Why not?
ROSEMARY:	The drinks are so expensive. You'd be penniless after one day.

66

ENA:	Really! You'd think I was a drunkard!
ROSEMARY:	Ai'd never think THET, dear. You hold your drink wonderfully well. Ai remember you at Brenda Spendlove's party . . . Mind you, Ai guessed you'd had enough when you fell flat on your back.
TOM:	(HURRIEDLY) Well, what about this holiday of ours?
ROSEMARY:	Holiday? Oh yes. Look, Ai've just remembered where you can have a nice holiday and it's only £100 a week for two.
TOM:	(EXCITED) Tell us, where is this place?
IAN:	Excuse me. I couldn't help overhearing. Where can we have this holiday?
ROSEMARY:	In a two-berth caravanette at Portobello.

Ballhead

A Varied Career

JOHN BALLHEAD, that singularly articulate Glaswegian, strenuously denies that he is a "celebrity", even
though he has appeared on television more than once.

"I have simply been able for to make use of some of
the talents which providence has so kindly gave me," he
says.

The following series of interviews reveal a few of the
facets of Mr. Ballhead's extraordinarily varied career.

Calendar Manufacturer

INTERVIEWER: Mr. Ballhead, you have become well-known for making and selling calendars. Is this a lucrative occupation?

BALLHEAD: It is not only lucrative but it also pays very well.

INTERVIEWER: But I'm told you don't put photographs of pretty girls on your calendars.

BALLHEAD: Oh no, I don't go in for anything like that. Ackchally, my calendars are noted for their unattractive pictures. That is why people are clamouring to purchase them.

INTERVIEWER: Do you mean to say that people want calendars with unattractive pictures on them?

BALLHEAD: Definately, definately! You see, some time ago a certain film star displayed her charms on a calendar. This, I regret for to say, had the most gravest effect on industrial productativity.

INTERVIEWER: Why was that?

BALLHEAD: Well, business men who possessed these calendars found that they could not remove their gazes from the torso, limbs and other features of this pre-possessing young lady. You can imagine what happened.

INTERVIEWER: What . . . er . . . DID happen?

BALLHEAD: These industrial typhoons looked and day-dreamed of dates of a kind not shown on the calendar. As a result work remained undone, important letters was left unwrote and vital contracts were lost. In fact, things reached such a critical crisis that something had to be did. So I decided that, instead of a pin-up calendar, I would place on the market a heid-doon calendar.

INTERVIEWER: A heid-doon calendar?

BALLHEAD: Yes . . . Every time you look at the picture on it you put your heid doon. This, of course, is a great boon to gents who is too partial to feminine beauty.

INTERVIEWER: And what kind of pictures do you have on your . . . er . . . heid-doon calendars?

BALLHEAD: Well there is a large and expansive selection of these pictorial scunners. One of my most highly successful calendars bears a simple study of an income tax inspector scowling at some person's tax return.

INTERVIEWER: Not a pleasant sight, I agree.

BALLHEAD: One business gent requested me to provide him with an even more revolting calendar. He wanted it to be so unattractive that he could not bear to even glance at it. So I produced a calendar that made him turn pale when he set eyes on it. From the moment he hung it up in his office his head was bent over his work. Each day he had to get his secretary to tell him the date.

INTERVIEWER: What WAS the picture that so terrified him?

BALLHEAD: A large photographic portrait of his mother-in-law with a gumboil.

INTERVIEWER: Incredible! But, Mr. Ballhead, why don't you have on your calendars some of the sights of Scotland?

BALLHEAD: Oh but I HAVE did that. I have just produced a calendar which bears a picture of one of the most frightening sights that has ever been saw in this country. It is designed to make business gents stop day-dreaming about pin-up damsels and work harder.

INTERVIEWER: And what does this frightening picture show?

BALLHEAD: Mrs. Thatcher and Mr. George Younger in an office full of Scottish rates assessors.

Biographer

INTERVIEWER: Biographies of famous people always make fascinating reading. In the book, "Secrets of Three Centuries", just published, are revealed many remarkable and hitherto unknown aspects of the lives of a wide range of historical figures. With me now is the author . . . John Ballhead, how were you able to unearth such a mass of new and what I can only call sensational material about celebrated men and women?

BALLHEAD: Well, I felt it was incumbent on me to give the matter much cogitation. You see, I have always been a vapid reader of biographies. But I became aware of a certain deficiency in most of these life stories.

INTERVIEWER: What was that?

BALLHEAD: There was no dampt life about them.

INTERVIEWER: And you wanted to change that?

BALLHEAD: You have hit the proverbial nail on the napper. I decided that the time had came for me to take up my pen and give these celebrated characters a much more trendier image.

INTERVIEWER: A trendier image? How did you arrive at your rather startling conclusion that Florence Nightingale was really Disraeli in drag?

BALLHEAD: To me it was obvious. You must remember that Disraeli was the Danny le Rue of his day. So, to ingratiatate himself with Queen Victoria, he attired himself in a crinoline and bonnet, took the nom dee plume "Florence Nightingale", and inventit tents for soldiers. Soon he became known as "The Lady with the Camp".

INTERVIEWER: Hmmm . . . I didn't know that . . . Now, on Page 296 of your book you refer to Thomas Carlyle as "The Rage of Chelsea". Shouldn't that read "The SAGE of Chelsea"?

BALLHEAD: No, no, "RAGE" is quite correct. To let you understand, Tommy Carlyle had a flat off the King's Road and was never out of the boutiques. Accordionly, inspired by the dolly birds he encountered there, he wrote "Great Expectations". Alas, these expectations came to nothing and Carlyle became, as we say in literry circles, biling mad.

INTERVIEWER: "Great Expectations"? Surely that was Dickens?

BALLHEAD: That is so. Carlyle was in a dickens of a rage. After that he immigrated to the Lake District and it was there he wrote his No 1 pome, "The Daffodils" . . . "When all at one-t I seen a host, a shower of golding daffodils, fluttering and . . . er . . . fluttering". . . Who can forget those unmortal lines?

INTERVIEWER: But wasn't the poem you refer to written by . . .

BALLHEAD: I know, I know. You are going to say it was wrote by Mrs. Barbara Cartland. That, I may say, is a complete pharmacy. Mrs. Cartland was interestit only in the bees that were perambulating round said daffodils. In fact, while Tommy Carlyle was occupied with the composure of his pome Mrs. Cartland was busy inventing her magical honey tonic. The first jar of this went to Mr. Terry Wogan, thus ensuring his life-long longevity and the gratitude of the entire British nation.

INTERVIEWER: Yes . . . Can we turn now to Chapter 10 which is devoted to Mrs. Lily Langtry. I was surprised to read your description of her as a strip-tease artiste who moved in the very highest circles.

BALLHEAD: Indeed she did. She revolved in high circles and low circles while performing her act. One night the playboy, Billy Gladstone, asked her for a keepsake. He said, "Give me your jersey, Lily." And Jersey Lily she remained till the termination of her career.

INTERVIEWER: Wasn't there a bearded gentleman who evinced great interest in Lily Langtry?

BALLHEAD: Aw, no doubt you are referring to Lloyd George.

INTERVIEWER: No, no, not Lloyd George. Anyway, he didn't have a beard.

BALLHEAD: I regret to say I must contradict you. He possessed an imitation beard which he put on when he visited Mrs. Langtry. And, of course, she wore a false beard when she paid her nocturnial visits to Lloyd George. On these occasions she used an assumed name — "Bernard Shaw."

INTERVIEWER: Good heavens, you're surely not implying that Bernard Shaw was Mrs. Langtry!

BALLHEAD: Well it has never been proved that he wasn't . . . Anyway, Mrs. Langtry gave some great parties. The conversation at these was brilliant. One evening Lloyd George emitted a bonn mott that has passed into our language. "Lily," he said, "You are A1 at Lloyd's!" Big Oscar Wilde fell about laughing. "I wish I had said that!" he observed to his pal, Somersault Maughan. Quick as a flash Somersault ryposted, "Oscar, you're away with the fairies!"

INTERVIEWER: I must say I never realised that Wilde and Maugham were contemporaries.

BALLHEAD: They got the name of it . . . but I regard these matters as private.

INTERVIEWER: You have an interesting theory about the death of Mussolini. You say, and I quote from Page 793 of your book, "Mussolini and his mistress, Signorina Pistachio were not lynched and hung up by the heels in a city square. Now, in the first place, was the woman's name not "Petacci"?

BALLHEAD: No, definately "Pistachio". She was nuts about Mussolini. Indeed it was this lady who helped him to escape. When he and she got to the square she invaigled a humble peasant and his wife into taking their place. "Just hang about there till we come back," she said. Then, without furder ado, Mussolini and she hurried off.

INTERVIEWER: And you say he escaped?

BALLHEAD: Yes . . . Later he was smuggled into Britain in a barrel of chianti. It wasn't long before he secured a post with British Rail. His task was to get the trains to run on time.

INTERVIEWER: And did he manage it.

BALLHEAD: No, it was too much for him. He flew back to Italy, gave himself up and was hanged.

Guru

INTERVIEWER: One of the newest religious movements in Britain is headed by a truly remarkable sage and philosopher . . . I talked with him in his temple . . . Guru, I understand that, for a long time, you have been a believer in Buddhism.

BALLHEAD: No, no . . . I am afraid that you are labouring under an interdenominational misapprehension. The movement of which I am spirituous leader is termed "Broodism".

INTERVIEWER: "BROODISM"?

BALLHEAD: That is correct. I evolvulatit this movement entirely on my tod. You see, for many years I have been very partial to brooding. Even as a child I would sit and brood over such things as ice cream, skelps on the ear and precocious small females or, as we termed them fly wee Lolitas. But after I had grew to manhood this changed diagnostically.

INTERVIEWER: In what way exactly?

BALLHEAD: I found myself brooding over the price of a pint, Mrs. Thatcher, Scottish rates, district councillors and other integral factotums of life.

INTERVIEWER: You believe there is solace to be found in communal brooding?

BALLHEAD: Oh, undubitably. Indeed we have became This Happy Brood.

INTERVIEWER: I was going to ask — have many people become . . . er . . . Broodists?

BALLHEAD: They certingly have. More people than ever before are brooding. Nowadays there is so much to brood about.

INTERVIEWER: Such as?

BALLHEAD: Well, you've got the Tory Party, of course, the fortunes pop stars make, President Reagan, income tax, public spending cuts, Miss Selina Scott and the Rangers and Hearts football teams.

INTERVIEWER: It seems that yours has become one of the most prominent of the sects.

BALLHEAD: Sex? Oh it plays a prominent part in our brooding. In fact we're always brooding about it.

INTERVIEWER: When I entered your temple this afternoon I couldn't help noticing that you were being caressed by a young lady. Is she one of your adherents.

BALLHEAD: Indeed she is. Sister Amanda adheres very closely. You may have heard of the Close Brethern. Well she is one of the Close Sistern . . . Yes, overflowing with love.

INTERVIEWER: Do you and your followers go in for meditation?

BALLHEAD: Of course. We term this process B.B.C. Or, to give it its full designiation — belly button comtemplating.

INTERVIEWER: I have heard it said that you yourself practice levitation. You know, floating in the air without any visible means of support.

BALLHEAD: You heard correct. Without any undue modesty I may state that I am one of the most foremost levitationers in the country today. Ackchally this gift of mines was first noticed by a fellow-guru of my acquaintance, Big Harry Crishnur.

INTERVIEWER: The name sounds familiar.

BALLHEAD: Does it? Well anyway, Big Harry happended to drop in on me one night to borrow a stick of incense but when he looked into my temple I was nowhere to be saw. Completely dumbfounder-ated, he called "Art thou there, Guru? Art thou there, Dangerous Dan?"

INTERVIEWER: Why did he call you THAT?

BALLHEAD: He'd got me mixed up with another well-known celebrity, Dangerous Dan Guru . . . Well, Big Harry was unable to perceive me. He called out again,

"Where hast thou went to?" At that I responded, "Up here, Harry." Judge of his pertubulation when he looked up and observed that I was suspendit in the air above his cranium.

INTERVIEWER: Good gracious, you were in a state of levitation!

BALLHEAD: Such was the case. I was engaged in the practice of advanced broodology, brooding about that great actress, Joan Collins, the Sarah Bernard of our times. I was completely carried away.

INTERVIEWER: I take it that this was your first experience of levitation?

BALLHEAD: Not exackly. I suspectit I possessed the gift when, one morning, I lowered the kitchen pulley and hung upon it certain ceremonial vestments of mines, including my sacred vest, or simmit. These I had just washed in my ecclesiastical jawbox. Suddenly I was not only elevatit but wheeched with great veracity towards the ceiling.

INTERVIEWER: Amazing! . . . And was this levitational power of yours noticed when you were young?

BALLHEAD: Oh yes . . . I used to hang about pubs and float about dance halls.

INTERVIEWER: I see . . . Now, Guru, you believe in total passivity, don't you? I mean you don't like violence . . .

BALLHEAD: Violins? No, I prefer the big band sound.

INTERVIEWER: No, I was thinking of your passivity. Supposing someone became aggressive towards you, say a man jostled you in the street. I take it you would NOT retaliate?

BALLHEAD: No, I would endeavour for to persuade him of the badness of his ways and invite him to join me in meditation and contemplation of the love that flows all around us.

INTERVIEWER: But if the man became even more violent?

BALLHEAD: I'd give the bugger a kick on the arse.

STINKWEED
GIGANTICLIS

Horticulturist

INTERVIEWER: How did your career as a horticulturist begin, Mr. Ballhead?

BALLHEAD: It commenced when I was a diminutative wean. My mother insisted that I should tend her window-box. The first things I sowed was amnesia seeds.

INTERVIEWER: Er ... Don't you mean nemesia seeds?

BALLHEAD: No, amnesia seeds. They forgot to come up. It was then I discovered that I possessed unusual horticultural propensities.

INTERVIEWER: You mean you didn't have green fingers?

BALLHEAD: That is so. I found that I had the very reverse of green fingers. The moment I placed these digits of mines on seeds they refused to grow.

INTERVIEWER: That's remarkable! Did that not make you want to give up gardening?

BALLHEAD: Far from it! My interest in horticulture intensifictated ... Now I sell seeds that never grow.

INTERVIEWER: Have I got that right? You sell seeds that never produce anything? What's the idea of THAT?

BALLHEAD: The idea is obvious. You must realise that in the Spring thousands of people are going about sneezing their craniums off with hay fever. Is it any wonder then that these sufferers are anxious to purchase my special unproductive grass seed for their gardens?

INTERVIEWER: Unproductive grass seed!

BALLHEAD: Yes, it's quite simple. You just sow the seed and no grass appears. Thus hay fever is kept to a minewmum.

INTERVIEWER: But surely people are not going to sow FLOWER seeds that don't produce anything?

BALLHEAD: They certingly are! Don't you see? These never-growing seeds keep a garden tidy. My customers that prefer going to golf and bingo to gardening never need to gather up withered blooms, rake flower beds or do other menial tasks.

INTERVIEWER: Don't they have to weed their gardens?

BALLHEAD: Never! Not if they sow my non-generating weed seeds. And they don't have to waste time spraying and pruning rose bushes. My non-growing rose bushes obviates these horticultural chores. The idea for these came to me one morning as I surveyed my mother's cottage. No doubt you have heard the touching old ballad "Roses round the door make me love mother more."

INTERVIEWER: Yes, I have.

BALLHEAD: Well, I regret for to say that the roses that circumnavigated the door of my mother's abode made me love her LESS. She desired to leave the cottage and go for her usual morning refreshment, just a couple of rums and a pint of heavy. I observed that she was in a terrible temper.

INTERVIEWER: Why was that, Mr. Ballhead?

BALLHEAD: She intimated the cause of this to me. "Ah've a helluva thirst oan me," she said, "An' Ah canny get oot the hoose fur thae bliddy rose trees."

INTERVIEWER: And that was when you thought of developing non-growing rose bushes?

BALLHEAD: Precisely. My mother stated that if I did not do something about those obstructive roses round her door she herself would plant something.

INTERVIEWER: What was she thinking of planting?

BALLHEAD: Her foot up ma bahookie.

INTERVIEWER: I see . . . Mr. Ballhead, it seems you've had nothing but success with your non-productive seeds and bushes.

BALLHEAD: Well, not exackly. I had one somewhat

regrettable failure. It concerned the Giant Pong Flower or, to give it its botaniacal name, Stinkweed Giganticus. Soon after I sowed a large quantity of those stinkweed seeds something came up.

INTERVIEWER: Ah, so the stinkweed came up!

BALLHEAD: No, the sanitary inspector.

The Champion

INTERVIEWER: My guest tonight John Ballhead, the new World Champion Dumpling-Flinger . . . John, how does it feel to have flung a dumpling further than any other living person?

BALLHEAD: It is highly gratificating. But, to tell you the truth, I did not expect to win the dumpling-flinging championship.

INTERVIEWER: Why was that?

BALLHEAD: An accident during training had almost rendered me horse dee combat. I was about to fling a practice dumpling when, all of a sudden, it disintiagratit.

INTERVIEWER: Did that affect your flinging arm?

BALLHEAD: No, not my arm. To let you understand . . . Under National Dumpling-flinging rules dumplings when flung has to be piping hot. So, when this defective dumpling disintiagratit, burning portions of same was hurled in all directions. As luck would have it a large daud landed on my anatomy. For ten days I was unable to sit down.

INTERVIEWER: But despite that you continued to train?

BALLHEAD: As soon as the breid poultice was removed. Us dumpling-flingers has to face the risk of a dumpling exploding or bursting out of its cloth, or clootie as we call it.

INTERVIEWER: Doesn't that sort of thing put you off the sport?

BALLHEAD: Never! The flagrant aroma of the steaming monsters as they wheech through the air and the eminence of danger provides an atmosphere that is absolutely unresistable.

INTERVIEWER: How did you happen to take up dumpling-flinging?

BALLHEAD: It was wrote in the stars that I should do so. I have grew up with dumplings. My mother made them all the time, in fact, uncessantly. In my home we ett nothing but dumplings.

INTERVIEWER: Nothing but dumplings!

BALLHEAD: That is correct. Before my father passed away he had consumed 1296 of these gargantuacious delicacies. The cause of death was statit to be "dumplinitis". The post mortem revealed that, in medical parliance, he had became "ferr stappit".

INTERVIEWER: I would have thought that that would have put you off eating dumplings.

BALLHEAD: As a matter of fact it did. On the day my father was laid to rest my mother consoled herself by making a very large dumpling. As she placed it upon the tea table I realised that I had went and took the most strongest scunner to dumplings.

INTERVIEWER: How did you react?

BALLHEAD? Withiut no hesitation I picked up the steaming twelve-pounder and flung it out the window. Such was the height it attained that reports of an unidentified flying object was received from near and far. Experts climbed to the top of Ben Lomond and established without no doubt that it was my mother's dumpling.

INTERVIEWER: So that was the start of your sporting career?

BALLHEAD: Indeed it was. Soon I was visited by none urrer than the President of the Association of Scottish Dumpling-Flingers. "Never," he said, "have I knew of a dumpling being threw so far." Then he insisted that I compete in the Scottish Dumpling-Flinging Championships.

INTERVIEWER: Of course, you won that championship.

BALLHEAD: I did, and after that I captained the British team at the Dumpling-Flinging

Olympics in Washington, D.C. . . . The D.C. I understand, stands for "Dumpling Contest" and refers to the American Presidential Election.

INTERVIEWER: And it was in Washington you won the Golden Dumpling Medal.

BALLHEAD: That is so . . . But that brings back a sad memory to me.

INTERVIEWER: A SAD memory?

BALLHEAD: Yes, it could not be more poignanter. It so happened that I had took a strong notion to a young lady, Miss Caroline McCloot.

INTERVIEWER: Ah, she was the British Ladies Champion Dumpling-Flinger.

BALLHEAD: She was. The grace with which she flung her dumplings caused me to become completely inflatulated with her. Alas, a disastrous countertemps ended our romance.

INTERVIEWER: What exactly was the . . . countertemps?

BALLHEAD: It happened after Caroline McCloot had flung her final dumpling. She lay back on the grass and intimated that she was utterly wabbit. The time had now came for me to fling for the Golden Dumpling Medal. Great was the tension as I bent down to pick up the steaming brown globe. The starter blew his burrle and I flung with all my might. Five seconds later I realised that I had made the most grevious error.

INTERVIEWER: What had you done?

BALLHEAD: Instead of the dumpling I had took hold of Miss McCloot's cranium and flung her half-a-mile. Never will I forget her cry as she shot heid-first into a dustbin.

INTERVIEWER: Good heavens! Was she injured?

BALLHEAD: No, but the dustbin was badly damaged. You can imagine my discomfurniture as I hurried to apologise to her. I am sorry for to say that she refused to listen. She likened me to a big pudden and requested that I should go and get knotted.

INTERVIEWER: So your romance was over.

BALLHEAD: Dead as the proverbial doornail. After that Caroline McCloot gave up dumpling-flinging and sunk very low. In fact, she went into politics. Strangely enough her political career took her into the Land of Dumplings.

INTERVIEWER: Oh, and where is the Land of Dumplings?

BALLHEAD: Where d'ye think? The House of Commons.

STANLEY BAXTER'S SUBURBAN SHOCKER